Reflections from Pete's Pond

Other books by H. Palmer Hall:

Reflections from Pete's Pond

poems by H. Palmer Hall

Pecan Grove Press San Antonio, Texas

Copyright © 2007
by H. Palmer Hall

ISBN: 978-1-931247-48-1

Pecan Grove Press
Box AL
1 Camino Santa Maria
San Antonio, TX 78228

Acknowledgments

Some of these poems have appeared in *Salt River Review* and in *Ampersand Poetry Journal.* Most were shared with friends I have only met electronically at the Pete's Pond Bloggers' Cafe on the Wildcam Web Site.

This small book and these poems are dedicated to the good people who gather most evenings at the Bloggers' Cafe to discuss what they are seeing at Pete's Pond on the Mashatu Game Reserve in Botswana, Africa.

They have formed one of the most supportive communities in cyberspace.

About Pete's Pond

Pete Le Roux created the pond that bears his name as a way of protecting African wildlife from the poachers who hunted them along the Limpopo River in Botswana where they had to go to find adequate water. Pete's Pond, in the Mashatu Game Reserve, has become, thanks to a live videocam that broadcasts via satellite and is sponsored by the National Geographic Society, one of the most often visited spots on the internet. Thousands of people from all over the world view the pond daily at *http://ngm.com/wildcamafrica* except during Botswana's rainy season when the cam is taken down.

Contents

Sunset in Mashatu

for Nyala

In this bright ending of an African day
we see any color we can imagine, watch birds
fly quickly from north to south and back again:
dusky silhouettes of their deeper selves.
The water reflects the brilliance, shows
dark trees outlined against a flaring sky.

Later, more somber hues, a trace of violet
in deep oranges, a flash of neon green.
The sun, a white-hot wafer in the west,
drops beneath baobab and mashatu trees
and darkness rises, ascends from still waters.
A few birds cry over the pond, a single deer.

And then, there is only and ever night,
a solitary jackal walks along the shore,
stops, drinks, shrinks from the dangers
of an African night. We wait for the sun,
for the promise of morning, listen
to the skirring of insects, the last bird call.

Solitude

for Mary in Kansas City

A single bull elephant stands at the end
of a peninsula jutting out into the pond.
Behind him, between two trees, some animal
races to get some place we cannot know

But it is the elephant that demands attention:
why did he wander out to that point in the water?
why does he stand there and not some other where?
like some model: Bull Elephant, Flexible Trunk.

He trumpets, makes some moue of disgust,
turns his rear to the camera and watches
some smaller, faster thing dart from right
to left. And then emerge. A jackal followed

by more elephants. The jackal shrinks away,
darts faster than the cam can catch back
into heavy brush. The picture of solitude
remains. No companionship as the others

walk ponderously away. A solitary elephant
stands at the end of the peninsula. He turns,
trunk weaving back and forth, walks away.
His shadow paints the trees. Silence.

This Night

Darfur in the distance
(the cam not scanning)
For Indiana John

We are stuck in this one spot—
eyes focused in the dark on insects
and birds flying in artificial light.
An impala races by, headed somewhere.
I listen, hear the roars of a lion
the haunting howls of jackals.

We learn, in detail, a simple arc
of the larger pond, see shadows,
hear water, know there is something
else if only our eyes could move just
a bit to the right where elephants
might be drinking or lions eating.

But the view is steady, unmoving.
We peer across the peninsula
into a far greater night marked
by howling and snarling, some
pathway into deeper darkness,
some Africa without the light.

Yawning in Tune

for Wolfkas

It is 5:09 in the morning
in Botswana and the same old fleas
do the same old dance
and will be followed by aunts

eloping and the ostreich
flaunting its dancing neck
uber alles. Lioning up in
elephabetical order we see Babe

Oon de Pond all deshabille
and Croc O'Dile the Irish gator
snapping at WorryWart
the selfish hawg—not waiting

for Halloween to illuminate
his Jackal Lantern.

5:10 in Botswana
and the live cam isn't.

The Lights Have Failed

for Anneleise

The biggest blur is almost of course
a maybe elephant, A kind of bloggiest
blog in a black black night.

The cam pans on, recording
the amorphous nature of an African night
without illumination. Has a lion come?

I have not heard a roar. Does a genet slink
down for a cool drink? Whatever
you want to think.

It is that kind of night, my dears, but
that's okay—for me at least…I have been
In the dark before today

about all sorts of things, this and that,
not just African cats. It will not be long
until noisy birds sing up the dawn

and the sun lights the pond. "The way
God meant it to be" as my great-
grandmother used to say.

That was after Mr. Edison had done his thing,
but even then she used only "natural" light,
was fast asleep by dark each night

She woke at the time the ibis calls in Botswana.
Sunlight, not a noisy bird or alarming clock,
signaled to her. She said God called.

But I am not so sure. Is that a jackal in the dark?
"Where jackals ought to be," she'd say. "But
I've seen them in the day," I'd say.

She just turns and goes, lit by candles, to her bed.
She's been gone for a long time—
"Passed away"—I miss her—

From before there was an internet, after electric lights
were a way of life. She used a wood stove.
"Like the one Mr. Franklin used."

As for me, Let there be light, natural or un—
To see what the twentieth century
Has to offer:

Elands and impala, lions and leopards,
Warthogs and wildebeests, genets and vervets
Giraffes and ostriches.

All these and so much more. And yet,
it is not just this century. They have roamed
here, on this arid plain, for a million years.

A Quiet Day at the Pond

for Gail in Arizona

The pond is calm today
not even a flea along the bank
but last night lions roared
and large fish lunged
for prey.
There ought to be lions.

The sky is clear.
Only a few birds dart
across the horizon.
A gentle breeze
rocks the vine.
There ought to be lions.

No elephants yet,
Not even a guinea hen
along the bank
The ostriches are away
Fatty is sleeping
Nothing moves.

There ought to be lions.

Untitled Clip 2

for jewllva

Untitled Clip 2 keeps running through my mind
and I wonder about Untitled Clip 1 and if there
is a Clip 3—also untitled—but the pond is full,
more so than last summer when Clip 2 was not just
untitled but that solitary elephant might well have been
as unsolitary then as the non-titular series of clips.

We have waited long and long for green water,
for a sense of that perhaps miss-titled "dark" continent
separated from the enlightened by a hunk of rock
that hawks insurance and beckons us to old beaches
and what passes for culture: a world of "stuff"
that now seems less essential than it had before.

Before? Before a Nile crocodile and guinea hens
played out a struggle more vital, more intense
than the blaring of horns and circling of taxis
on the Glorieta de Dos Rios. Did you see
the lion last night? Just for a moment and then
the cameras panned. One moment out of hours.

And yet, those hours spent watching trees and
empty banks and hearing clanking in the hide
beside the pond show something we cannot glean
from well-trafficked streets and highways,
from shopping malls and black tie parties.
Enough! We watch and wait again tonight.

First and Last

For Eleanor in New York City

I always try to stay awake until the first guinea
hen flashes across the screen. Red mornings
in Mashatu: water rippling and shadows growing.

It is about to happen: in the blackness,
the sky lightens and some small difference of gray
separates dark land from deepening sky.

The sounds of Africa, alive all night,
grow louder, skrees and squeaks, whistles and
warbling magnify the predawn land.

5 a.m. in Botswana, at Mashatu,
where sounds echo around a still pond
waiting for some new sunrise. Listen:

some grunting sound, some sharp whistle.
Would you walk along the shore, stride
out onto the peninsula? Big cats wait.

Something coughs, clears its throat. A twig
snaps. Some frightful rasp from a tree conjures
old nightmares...and yet, we see nothing now.

No camera sends images by satellite from the wild.
Pete's pond is silent and we are blind to it...
waiting, yet again, for a part from Johannesberg.

Still, imagination works, always, and elephants
continue to come to the pond and ostriches
scoop water into long, long throats. A jackal

yips and a giant owl perches on the peninsula...
this night, this long night when bats wheel
after insects glowing above a dark pond.

A Troubling Desire
For Betty in Michigan

We are of mixed minds—well, yes, no—
but I am thinking about storms over
the pond in Mashatu, in Botswana. See,

we want the animals healthy, well-fed,
to have a steady drinking supply, young
shoots growing on glowing green trees,

but we want them to come to the pond
and when rain fills low places, they drink there
until drought returns to Southern Africa.

So, yes, we want the animals happy, healthy,
well-fed, not thirsty, but we want them
where we can see them. Voyeurs of a sort,

we find it difficult to see inches of rain fall
over our favorite viewing grounds, don't
think, often, of how good this is for the animals.

We read of a dead giraffe and her young—
the mother too weak from hunger to give birth—
and recoil. We know we should pray for rain.

And we do. We are, and I say this thoughtfully,
good people. It's just that, well, sometimes,
deep down, we want to, need to, see lions.

We want to see giraffes, ostriches and jackals
and wart hogs and antelope and baboons. We want
to see so much, but.... Ah, let the rains come.

Falling Rain

for Nancy in Indiana

Rain falls on the Mashatu Game Reserve,
wakes Afke in her tent. We see lightning
spark the sky into flaring balls and sheets
of rain sweep across the pond. And yet,

it is not the right season. It should be dry.
Dust should be blowing along the shore.
Things have turned around, upside down
in the arid country that is Botswana.

No elephants come to drink, no jackals—
they have found water everywhere.
And yet—a giraffe died giving birth,
weakened by long drought, they suspect.

Perhaps even this rainy week came too late.
Perhaps there can not be too much water
to drink, too much grass to eat. This is
the animals' communion, their life. Rain falls.

Giraffes and Impala

for Katie Girl

Giraffes and impala stand in a thunder storm,
eyes turned away from the rain.

The little raft cam churning across the pond,
gives us a wonderful view of the whole place.

We see the hide and Fatty on the bank
and in the water large fish create ripples.

The subtle colors of the evening in Botswana:
stark, arid, cobalt blue skies and calm waters

A variety of birds, from ducks atop the tall, stark tree
to doves scratching for food

And, finally, we are grateful for a cam that gives
us pleasure of the pond in color and at night.

Communion

For Mary in Kansas City

We drink and celebrate.
Rain brightens even
the darkest cityscape

Waterfalls leap brightly down
mountainsides and rainbows
arc above them.

Is it any wonder that
the elephant lowers his trunk
and flings sparkling water
high into the evening sky?

That impala and guineas
gather at Pete's Pond?
that wart hogs wallow?

Water is a holy thing—
a communion for all
not just for believers.

Let us drink, clink glasses,
lift them high and bright.
even the lions gather
for this liquid holiness.

Through the Screen

based on "There's a Hole in My Sidewalk" by Portia Nelson

for Lynty

1

I turn on the computer.

There is a darkness on the screen.

My eyes glaze over,

try to focus…nothing there.

It's the resolution.

Some strange animal moving.

2.

I turn on the computer again.

There are people talking.

Some humming and thumping sound.

My ears tune out.

I don't know why I try.

It is surely my fault.

A small animal moves away.

3.
I restart the computer.
The darkness is amorphous
It is alive
I lean closer, fall through.
My eyes are closed.

I do not know where I am.
No, they are not closed.
I cannot get out.

4.
The computer turns itself off.
I fall into a pond.
A lion roars.

A Villanelle for the Rainy Season

For Afke, cam operator at Pete's Pond

I love the pond when it is wild and green
even if few animals come to drink, unseen,
quenching thirst at some other watering hole.

No elephants today, no lioness, no waterbuck,
no vervets or baboons picking away at fleas. Still,
I love the pond when it is wild and green

because that color is the life force, sign of spring,
of water irrigating parched lands, allowing animals
to quench their thirst at other watering holes.

That color is the wild fluid, the source, creative juice
that brings liquid life to sing again and lets us all
quench our thirst at our own, different, watering holes.

Everything green and wet teems with growing life
and drinking deep keeps every living thing in grace.
So, quench your thirst at every watering hole and
love all ponds when they are wild and green.

For All the Bloggers at the Café

with many thank yous

I am not thankful most for Pete's pond, not at all,
but it is on my list of thank yous, as are you all
who cheerfully make the café a pleasant place
even when the pond disappears without a trace

because of terrorists in London or sun storms
or stormy weather in Botswana, all of us forlorn
because animals and birds and insects remain
when the cam is down and we would go insane

without the bloggers babbling brookish here
it would all be bleak, no pond, nothing to cheer.

Pecan Grove Press is an independent literary press that publishes, almost exclusively, **poetry** from all over the world. This year, the press is celebrating its twentieth birthday. Its logo, a bare pecan tree from the Pecan Grove at St. Mary's University, was designed by Dennis Peyton, then a student at the university. The press continues to publish one or two student poets each year. Pecan Grove Press is a member of the Council of Literary Magazines and Presses [CLMP]. To see a complete listing of its "in print" books, please visit the website at

http://library.stmarytx.edu/pgpress